Everyday Rituals

Gentle Practices for Mindful Living

Matthew Joseph Klein

ATMOSPHERICUS PRESS

Everyday Rituals: Gentle Practices for Mindful Living

Published by ATMOSPHERICUS PRESS, an imprint of ATMOSPHERICUS LLC. www.ATMOSPHERICUS.com.

ATMOSPHERICUS is a trademark of ATMOSPHERICUS LLC.

ISBN: 979-8-218-92163-7

This book is provided for educational and inspirational purposes only and is not medical, psychological, or legal advice.

Edition: First 2026

Printed in the United States of America

ATMOSPHERICUS PRESS books are available at special discounts for bulk purchases for sales promotions or corporate use. Special editions, including personalized covers, excerpts of existing books, or books with corporate logos, can be created in large quantities for special needs. For more information, contact premium sales at (786) 372-0369 or email press@atmosphericus.com.

Dedication

For my mother, Donna—your love has always been my home.

For my father, Michael—thank you for your strength, support, and

steady example.

And for Seksit—thank you for your gentle guidance, your comfort,

and for always being there, without hesitation.

How to Use This Book

This book is a companion for mindful living. You can read one reflection each day, or simply open to a page when you need a moment of calm.

Each page offers a short practice, affirmation, or principle you can gently incorporate into daily life.

• Find a quiet moment: Read the practice slowly, letting the words settle in your heart.

• Reflect: Pause for a few breaths to reflect on how the message applies to your life.

• Practice: If a page suggests an action (like breathing or observing), try it on the spot or during your day.

There are also special pages for the seasonal transitions of spring, summer, autumn, and winter. You might turn to these at the change of seasons for a simple ritual to honor nature's cycles.

Use the closing note for inspiration about the spirit behind these practices.

Above all, approach this book in whatever way feels comforting.
There is no right or wrong method.

Let it be a gentle guide, and enjoy the calm journey.

Everyday Practices and Reflections

Read slowly. Pause. Practice gently.

Mindful Breathing

One of the simplest rituals is to focus on your breath.
Find a comfortable position and allow your breathing to anchor you in the present.

Try this gentle practice:

Pause and inhale deeply: Close your eyes and take a slow, deep breath through your nose. Feel your lungs fill with air, allowing your belly to expand.

Exhale and relax: Breathe out gently through your mouth. As the air leaves your body, imagine any tension flowing out with it.

Continue with awareness: Take a few more mindful breaths, paying attention to the sensation of air entering and leaving. With each exhale, let your shoulders drop and your mind soften.

Whenever life feels rushed or stressful, return to your breathing.
Even a few conscious breaths can bring you back to a calm center.

Mindful breathing is a portable sanctuary – a ritual you carry within, available at any moment.

Body Awareness

Take a moment to gently connect with your body. Our bodies often hold stress or unnoticed sensations. By doing a simple scan, you invite relaxation and presence.

Sit or lie down comfortably, and bring your attention from head to toe. Notice any areas of tightness – your jaw, shoulders, or back – and soften them.

Imagine a warm light moving through you, releasing each spot of tension in turn. Feel your feet against the floor and the weight of your body being supported by the earth.

Silently note: "Here I am, in this body, breathing." By listening to your body with kindness, you cultivate ease and wholeness.

Living in the Present

So much peace can be found in the here and now. Often, our minds drift to the past or race into the future. In this ritual, gently guide your attention back to what is happening now.

Notice the sounds around you, the colors and light in your space, or the simple feeling of your hands resting in your lap.

Remind yourself: This moment is your life. By fully experiencing the present, you release the burdens of what has already happened and the worries of what has yet to come.

A classic mindfulness reminder: do not dwell in the past or dream of the future. Be present with what is here now.

Cultivating Gratitude

Gratitude is a gentle practice of acknowledging the goodness in our lives. Bring to mind something you are thankful for – perhaps a warm cup of tea, a kind message, or the fact that you woke up today.

Allow appreciation to arise without rushing. Notice how it feels in the body. Often the heart feels lighter or warmer.

By recognizing small blessings, we shift from lack to abundance. Even on difficult days, there is often something worthy of appreciation.

A simple ritual: each evening, name three small things you can honestly be grateful for.

The Joy of Generosity

Giving can be a source of true happiness. This practice encourages small acts of kindness, expecting nothing in return.

Try this ritual: each day, find one opportunity to give – your time, a listening ear, or a simple favor. Do it mindfully, with care.

When we light a lamp for someone, it brightens our own path as well.

Loving-Kindness

This practice comes from the metta tradition of sending loving-kindness to oneself and all beings.

Sit quietly and repeat soft phrases: "May I be happy. May I be peaceful. May I be healthy. May I live with ease."

Then extend these wishes outward: to someone you love, to acquaintances, to strangers, and finally to all beings.

As you practice, notice your heart growing more expansive and tender. Loving-kindness can dissolve anger and soften isolation.

Compassionate Heart

Compassion is the natural response of the heart when confronted with suffering – our own or others'.

Acknowledge what is difficult. Breathe in with understanding, and breathe out sending comfort.

You might use phrases: "May you be free from pain. May you find peace."

A timeless reminder: hatred is not healed by hatred. It is healed by love.

Joyful Appreciation

Joy can be cultivated – especially the joy that shares in the happiness of others. This quality is sometimes called appreciative joy.

Try this ritual: think of someone experiencing something good. Smile and silently wish them well. Let yourself feel genuinely glad for them.

This practice counteracts envy and comparison.
It reminds us that goodness is not a competition.

Also practice appreciation for your own small joys.
Pause to savor them.

Deep Listening

Listening deeply is a gift. Set the intention to listen without interrupting, judging, or rehearsing your reply.

When someone speaks, give full attention to their words and the feeling beneath them. Let silence be okay.

You can also practice deep listening with yourself. When feelings arise, pause and listen to what your heart is asking for.

Kind Speech

Before speaking – especially in frustration – pause and ask:
Are my words true? Are they necessary? Are they kind?

Try a daily ritual of offering a few kind words to someone.
A sincere thank-you, a compliment, or "I appreciate you."

If anger rises, breathe. Speak slowly. Or wait until you feel calmer.

Patience

Patience is a quiet form of strength.
It is the ability to stay calm when things take longer than we'd like.

Next time you are waiting – in traffic, in a line, or for an outcome
–   use it as a cue to breathe and observe.

Silently repeat: "It's okay. I can be at ease here."
Watch impatience like clouds passing by.

Patience with people grows from compassion and the recognition that
everyone is doing the best they can in that moment.

Forgiveness

Holding grudges can feel like carrying a stone in the heart.
Forgiveness is gently putting that stone down.

This practice is not excusing harm. It is freeing yourself from
the ongoing cost of resentment.

In a quiet moment, bring to mind someone (or yourself) toward
whom you carry resentment or regret. Then, if you are ready, say:
"I forgive you. I release this burden."

Forgiveness can be gradual. Repeat as needed.
Each time you do, you make room for peace.

Embracing Impermanence

Everything changes. This truth can help us appreciate the present and soften our grip.

Notice how a flower blooms and fades, how weather shifts, how emotions change over hours.

A small ritual: feel the warmth of a drink knowing it will cool. Savor the taste knowing it will pass.

Impermanence is also hope. Pain fades. Seasons turn. New beginnings arrive.

Letting Go

As we clear clutter to feel more spacious, we can also clear the heart by releasing what no longer serves us.

Ask: "What am I holding that I no longer need to carry?"
On an exhale, imagine loosening your grip.

Try saying softly: "I let this go." Repeat as often as needed.

Peace grows in proportion to our willingness to release.

Contentment

Contentment is the art of feeling satisfied with what is here
– right now.

Pause and take stock of what already supports you: shelter, food, breath, the ability to move and learn.

Try this phrase: "I have enough. I am enough."

Notice the relief it can bring.

Contentment does not cancel goals. It simply refuses to postpone peace until everything is perfect.

Simplicity

Simplicity means reducing clutter and complication in our environment and in our mind.

Choose one area to streamline – your schedule, your phone use, or a physical space in your home.

As you clear outer clutter, notice how inner clutter often calms too.

A simple ritual: tidy one small surface each day, and affirm: "I create space for what matters."

Gentle with Yourself

In practicing kindness toward the world, include yourself. Treat yourself as you would a dear friend.

Notice self-criticism. Pause. Place a hand on your heart and say: "I'm doing my best, and that is enough."

If you are tired, allow rest without guilt. If you make a mistake, learn and begin again.

Non-Judgmental Awareness

This practice invites you to experience moments without immediately labeling them good or bad.

As sensations arise, simply note them: "tightness," "warmth," "thought," without adding a story.

Try it on a walk or during a meal. Experience taste and sight without commentary.

Open awareness creates space for wiser responses.

Equanimity

Equanimity is balance: a steady mind in the face of life's highs and lows.

Enjoy what is pleasant without clinging.
Meet what is difficult without collapsing.

Use this phrase: "This is how it is right now. It will change."

A brief ritual: imagine yourself like a mountain, calm and rooted, as weather passes around you.

Moments of Stillness

Stillness is a mini-retreat you can take anytime.
Sit for a few minutes in silence. Let the world's noise fall away.

You do not need to achieve anything. Just breathe. Just be.

Try "stillness breaks" during the day: a pause in the car,
a bench in the sun, a quiet corner before a meeting.

Mindful Eating

Turn eating into a calming ritual. Before a meal, pause and appreciate the food and the conditions that brought it to you.

Eat a bit more slowly. Notice flavor, texture, and aroma.
Put down your utensil between bites.

If your mind wanders, return to the sensory experience.

Even one mindful meal a day can transform your relationship with food.

Mindful Walking

Walking can become a meditation. Walk a bit more slowly than usual and feel each step: heel, sole, toes.

Synchronize breath and steps if you like. Let thoughts arise and pass, then return to the movement.

Peace is not only found in stillness. It can be found in each mindful step.

The Sacred Pause

When you feel overwhelmed, intentionally pause before reacting.
Stop for one breath and name what is present: "stress is here."

In that pause, ask: "What do I need right now?"
Another breath, water, a step outside, a slower response.

Small pauses break the chain of reactivity and restore freedom.

Beginner's Mind and Wonder

Approach life with fresh eyes. Pretend you are encountering an ordinary object or routine for the first time.

Notice new details: sound, color, texture, light. Let yourself feel a moment of wonder.

A daily ritual: identify one small "miracle" and pause to appreciate it.

Nature's Lessons

Nature is a quiet teacher. Even a single tree or a slice of sky can offer calm and insight.

Step outside or gaze out a window. Feel the air. Notice movement and stillness.

Let nature remind you: life changes, renews, and begins again, without force.

Morning Intention

Before you reach for your phone, take a few quiet breaths.
Set a simple intention for the day ahead.

Examples: "Today, I will be kind." "Today, I will be patient."
"Today, I will notice small joys."

Let this be a seed, not a pressure.
During the day, return to it as a touchstone.

Evening Reflection

As the day ends, give yourself closure.
Sit quietly and take a few deep breaths.

Review the day gently. Notice what you are grateful for.
Acknowledge what was hard without judgment.

End with release: "The day is done. May I and all beings rest peacefully."

Then let the day go.

Observing Emotions

Emotions are visitors. The next time a strong emotion arises,
pause and name it: "There is sadness."

Notice where it lives in the body.
Breathe gently into that area with kindness.

Let the emotion be present without feeding it with stories.
Watch it change and move in its own time.

Inner Light

Imagine a small warm light glowing in the center of your chest.
This represents your innate goodness and steadiness.

With each inhale, let it brighten.
With each exhale, let it radiate through your body.

Affirm quietly: "In my core, I am good. I am enough."

Planting Seeds of Goodness

Every action is a seed. When we plant kindness and wisdom, we tend the garden of our future.

Set an intention to plant at least one seed of goodness each day: a helpful act, patience in a hard moment, a sincere apology.

In the evening, reflect: "What seeds did I plant today?"
Then begin again tomorrow.

Seasonal Transitions and Rituals

Honor nature's cycles. Let the seasons teach you.

Spring – Renewal

Step outside and notice signs of new growth.
Breathe in the freshness and let the body feel the season's lightness.

Choose one area of life you want to refresh. A simple ritual: plant a seed (or tidy a space) as a symbol of beginning again.

Set a gentle intention: "May I grow in patience."
"May I welcome new opportunities."

Summer – Abundance and Light

Watch a sunrise or sunset.
Let the warmth of light remind you of life's generosity.

A ritual: light a candle in the evening and name what has ripened in your life, however small.

Share your abundance. Offer time, attention, or kindness as a way of embodying light.

Autumn – Letting Go

Observe leaves turning and falling.
Nature releases without bitterness.

Choose one thing to loosen your grip on.
Hold a leaf, breathe, and let it go as a symbol of release.

Declutter one small area. Notice the lightness that follows.

Winter – Rest and Reflection

Create a cozy space. Light a candle and sit quietly with the flame.

Use winter to rest and reflect. Journal once a week, or simply sit in silence for a few minutes each evening.

Trust the seasons.
Beneath stillness, new growth is gathering strength.

Closing Note

In these pages, we explored gentle practices inspired by timeless teachings. Many principles here echo wisdom shared freely across spiritual communities – mindfulness, compassion, impermanence, and balance.

Take what resonates. Adapt what you wish. There is no finish line – only the ongoing journey of returning to the present, opening the heart, and living with a little more care each day.

May you be well. May you be happy. May your life be peaceful.